THROWING THE BONES

Divination for the Modern Practitioner

Atalanta Moonfire

A modernistic and traditional way to celebrate and explore one of the oldest forms of spiritual guidance!

Throwing The Bones Divination for the Modern Practitioner

A modernistic and traditional
way to celebrate and explore one of the oldest
forms of spiritual guidance!

Atalanta Moonfire

Copyright 2020 Atalanta Moonfire, LLC

All rights reserved.

Project Staff:

Editor	Ashleah Hudson
Designer & Primary Photographer	Patrick Boone
Cover Design	Patrick Boone
Contributing Assistant	Sheri Rasko

Published by

Atalanta Moonfire, LLC

Monticelo, Georgia

AtalantaMoonfire.com

DEDICATION

To Tim, who I give my love and thanks for his support; to my parents for allowing me to be myself; and to my children, Chera and Daemion, and my grandson, Cooper, who have given me the courage and inspiration to create and manifest all of my dreams!

SPECIAL THANKS TO:

Sheri Rasko

Patrick Boone

Ashleah Hudson

Bill Bobo

Priestess Tiffany Lee

Sacred Moon Coven

TABLE OF CONTENTS

Introduction	9
The Account Of Throwing Bones	13
Ancestral Altar	17
Bones, Shells, & Curios	19
Meanings of Pieces & Tools	23
Getting Started & General Information	78
Personalizing Your Set	89
Preparation of Fresh Bones & Feet	94
Basic Beginner Reading	99
Other Readings	106
Conclussion	121
Resources	122
References	125
Personal Impressions	126

INTRODUCTION

Before we start, let me state that you do not have to be a Hoodoo (magic that was formed in the south during the slave trade times by combining a mixture of the various African beliefs) practitioner to throw the bones. This is the use of bones, shells, and curios to foretell future events and to give advice through your Ancestors and Spirit Guides.

My goal for this book is to provide a guide that adapts to this ever-changing world and that quickly teaches the art of throwing bones (also known as casting bones), as well as furnish a tool for fast and easy reference to keep on hand when needed. Let's get rid of the stigma that bone reading is hard to do and intimidating! We are here to change that!

The following is a collection of information I have gathered through verbal instruction and research combined with my own experiences and techniques.

There are many forms of divination, which means the practice of communicating with Ancestors, Spirit Guides and loved ones that have passed away in order to advise and see current events as well as future occurrences. This is usually, but not always, done with the help of divination tools. The most common forms of divination are tarot reading (examining cards and how they fall in a particular layout), dowsing (the use of a pendulum), crystal gazing (looking into a crystal ball), palmistry (reading the lines of the hand), rune casting (reading small items marked with the Elder Futhark or Old Norse Alphabet), and, "throwing" bones (using bones, and/or shells and curios to read their placement after a throw on a mat).

It does not stop there. Some strange and unusual forms of divination are scattering pebbles, observing atmospheric pressure, analyzing footprints, and even studying the Querent's feces. Yes – you read that correctly.

Personally, my favorite forms of divination are tarot reading and throwing bones. For over twenty-five years, I read only tarot. Then, about nine years ago, I was introduced to "throwing the bones" while attending a workshop at a Pagan festival. After participating in the class, I knew I was bitten by the bug. Tarot had been my divination practice of choice for so long, but at this workshop my eyes were open to a whole new world. Immediately after returning home, I began studying anything and everything pertaining to the bones I could find. A few years passed and I was teaching workshops at pagan events and teaching one-on-one and group classes. I also preformed personal readings and event appearances on a regular basis.

One problem I faced as a beginner student was that there was not much information regarding the specifics of bone throwing, and I had so many questions. Bone reading is primarily learned by traditions handed down verbally. Yes - I found a few published books (very few) and some various online articles, but none of which really had the detailed instruction I desired. I learned that throwing bones is a very personal form of divination. There is no "wrong way" to carry out a reading; however I discovered that teaching classes which established a basic process in the beginning allows the student to immediately execute readings, while still learning what the pieces represent which can be overwhelming at first. Other reading variations or techniques can be learned as the student becomes comfortable with meanings and confidence is gained.

<u>Throwing The Bones Divination for the Modern Practitioner</u> is for those who want to learn the art of throwing and reading the bones. In this text, we will dive into all aspects of this craft, including the account of bone throwing as we know, creating your Ancestral Altar, piece meanings, tools, preparation of fresh bones, and many various types of readings.

I hope this book will give you a very modern way to celebrate and explore one of the oldest forms of divination and make you fall in love with throwing bones like I have!

THE ACCOUNT OF THROWING BONES

We do not know where and when bone throwing originated exactly. We do, however, know that throwing the bones goes back to ancient times. Many variations and types are found throughout the world. To give you an idea of the diversity, I will touch on a few.

When considering the bones, most people think of Hoodoo and Voodoo. However, it is practiced in many religions and cultures. It is not just practiced in Africa, where the Sangoma is equivalent to the United States Native American Shaman. Northwestern cultures used bones to foresee events as well as advise before battle. Asia and North America are also leaders in the use of bones for divination.

We do not have much information on the history of throwing bones due to most cultures handing down the information by word of mouth and firsthand experience. Much like witchcraft, up until now, through acceptance and internet research this practice was only handed down through verbal communication. In South Africa, the Sangoma – the traditional healers of the Zulu, Swazi, Xhosa, and Ndebele tribes – continue to practice throwing bones only by way of verbal communication.

The Sangoma use bones as divination in more than one way. They not only use them as a means for foreseeing future events, but also use them to heal the ill and injured. Generally, the Sangoma call on the Ancestors of the afflicted as well as their own, then throw the bones, which are called the dingaka. The dingaka are four bones decorated on one side with color. Sometimes, after the Sangoma has become more seasoned with the practice, shells are added to the throw. Either the Sangoma or patient may do the throw. The Ancestors control how they land, and then through interpretation and connection with them, the Sangoma determines what the illness or injury is and how it may be treated. The Sangoma then throws the dingaka again to determine if they can help the patient. If the answer is yes, the information from the throw gives instruction on how to treat the patient. In some traditions, the dingaka are the actual practitioners known as Dingaka tsa Setswana.

The people of Northwestern European cultures used runes, which were bones carved with symbols to represent letters, events and sacred places. The oldest runes were called Futhark bone runes. Although runes were used predominantly, actual bones were incorporated into their divination practice as well. Runes are still commonly read today.

In Egypt, Greece, and Italy, throwing bones was called cleromancy and was the use of astragalus bones (the back anklebones of sheep, goats, deer, and oxen). In Italy and Greece, divination was practiced by the wealthy alongside the lower class to determine future events and give advice. It played a major role in Greek religion and was taught by being verbally passed on by individual to individual. In Greece, they are still used and are called hucklebones or knucklebones. Games called "Five Stones" and "Omilla" are still played by children today in all three countries in order to see about a happy future.

During the Shang Dynasty of China, oracle bones (also called dragon bones) were used. They were usually made of the shoulder blades of oxen or turtle shells due to their flat nature. Questions were carved or painted on one side, then heat was applied by a hot poker or fire. After the bone or shell cracked, it was removed from the heat and cooled. The cracks and marks were then interpreted for the answer to the question. Sometimes, symbols were marked on the bones and shells instead of questions. The same process above was used, and the interpretations were taken as advice for future events.

Another technique for reading bones includes cooking the bones down to where they have no meat left on them, then interpreting the markings that is left on the bone. One other technique, Oracle Bones, is when the bones are heated until they crack, and the charred remains are left for interpretation. This is called "Divination by Scapulae".

In the Southern United States, reading bones is a combination of African, Southern Hoodoo, and Native American cultures. Through communication with the ancestors, they tell of current situations, give advice, provide answers to questions, and predict future events. For years, bone reading was learned by verbal communication. Only recently did the secret come out. Even though it is one of the oldest forms of divination, it did not gain its popularity in the United States until around 1954.

The form of casting bones in this book is similar to the shamanic style, but it incorporates my learning and the research I have done over the years on modern ways of using bones, shells, and curios as taught to me.

ANCESTRAL ALTAR

The Ancestral Altar is a key component in throwing bones. It is a sacred space where offerings can be made and communication with the Ancestors can be done properly. It is also a significant place to learn the meanings of your bones as it helps you connect with your Ancestors, Deities, and Spirit Guides. Your Ancestors are those family members that have passed away, your Deities are those of whom you pray to, and your Spirit Guides are those enlightened spirits who give you guidance in life. It is important to introduce your bones to them because they influence you and are the key components to your readings. Also, the Ancestral Altar is a dedicated space where your bones should be stored when not in use or on you.

Your altar does not have to be complicated. A shelf with photos, candles, and incense is perfectly acceptable. You might want to set up an elaborate altar with items that represent your Ancestors, incense, candles, photos, and the like. Place a small glass or bowl of clean water on your altar to help connect with your Ancestors and Spirit Guides. There is no set guide in creating your space other than it is very important to not put photos or representations of living people on your Ancestral Altar.

Other than that, be creative! Include what brings you closer to your Spiritual Workers.

Your Ancestral Altar is a sacred space. It is best not to put it in your bedroom, but if you do, keep it covered out of respect.

Remember to maintain your Ancestral Altar. Keep it clean and provide offerings often. Some popular offerings are rum, whiskey, favorite foods of your Ancestor(s), and tobacco. The rule of thumb is if it is something they liked in life, more than often, it is something they will like as an offering.

Use your altar for prayer. Use it to serve as a space for your divination tools. Use it to connect with your Ancestors.

Below are some examples of simple altars:

BONES, SHELLS, & CURIOS

Throwing bones helps us access psychic energy and improve intuition. It is also a way for our Ancestors to communicate with us. We can use bones to connect with Ancestors, Deities and Spirit Guides. Through these connections, we can predict future events as well as give advice when needed. For the sake of this book, we refer to all items used as "pieces" or "bones."

Bone sets are as diverse as the many people who read them. Each is personalized by their owner and usually contains bones, shells, curios and other little trinkets. You may purchase bones or randomly find pieces that speak to you. If you purchase bones, be sure to only purchase from a company that is "cruelty free." If collecting on your own, you must clean them properly (as is mentioned in Chapter 7). Either way is acceptable and will make the set "yours."

A beginner or starter set usually consists of 16 – 20 pieces and costs between $40 - $60. These usually include a raccoon baculum, muskrat mandible(s), a cat bone, a snake vertebrae, a shark's tooth, a skull, a deer antler slice, a thimble, a button, two wooden beads, a chicken bone, a dice, two large cowrie shells, a cat's eye shell, a coin, a bell, a ring, and a buckeye nut. A deluxe set includes 20 - 60 pieces and includes the starter set as well as additional representations. These sets start around $80 and can run up to $150 or more.

Sets may contain an unlimited number of pieces as they begin to grow. My personal set contains over two hundred pieces and is still growing! You may also consider having a smaller set for travel with only the basics for on-the-go readings. Keep in mind that it is a travel set and much smaller than your collection. Include the same "subject pieces" (pieces that represent the main areas in our lives) and any other pieces that speak to you. If a subject comes up that you do not have a piece for, you may use a bone, shell, or bead to represent it. You may even want to consider adding that subject to your set!

Though love and finances are the most popular subjects Querents (the Questioner) ask about, it is imperative that you include all main topics:
Self (Querent), Health, Family as a Whole, Work & School, Children as a Whole, Projects & Activities, Friends as a Whole, Travel (Literally & Figuratively), Home & Hearth, Legal Matters, Love & Romance, Spirit Guide, Finances & Ancestors.

It is also important to have a starter piece, which provides you with a place to start after you read the piece that represents your Querent. A gem bracelet and Herkimer diamond are useful for guiding you to the most important aspects of the reading.

Meanings are mainly derived from handed down knowledge. Books, internet searches for animal representations, and personal intuition can provide you with other sources of meanings.

Also, it is important to mention here that if a piece is said to have one particular meaning, but you feel it represents something else, go with your gut feeling. For example, a snake bone or snakeskin usually means flexibility, strength, and transformation. To someone who might be afraid of snakes, the skin might mean fear. It is perfectly acceptable to change meanings to what resonates with you. We will discuss this further in the "Meanings" area following this chapter. Personally, as you will see, I use the traditional meanings when available. If the traditional meaning is not available, I make use of research and personal experience to create a meaning.

First, you will need pieces to represent people. Most times, shells or beads are used for this purpose. The most common people represented are the Querent, Significant Other, Children, and Friends. Of course, other people can be represented as needed.

When I first started reading, I used beads to represent my partner and me. For my children, I had little children charms (one boy and one girl). For my grandson, I used a little curio shaped like a child. I have now retired those and use beautiful little silver-plated shells to represent my immediate family and me.

Another idea is the use of worry dolls to represent the Querent and other people in the reading rather than shells or beads. I use worry dolls when I am doing multiple readings for others at events. They are a fun token for the Querent to take home as a souvenir, and they can be brought back and reused for future readings. We can use the dolls as they are already blessed and attached to the Querent. Of course, this works with shells and beads as well, but I have found the little dolls are most popular.

MEANINGS OF PIECES & TOOLS

Following is a list of the meanings I use when interpreting the bones. When available, I use the traditional meaning (the meaning passed down verbally through generations of the practice). When not available, I create a meaning through research as a guide or by using what the piece personally resonates with me.

Any piece facing down is considered "silent" and does not speak (is not read) in a reading unless otherwise noted.

Please also note that the pictures are examples from my personal collection and are only shown as examples. All pieces come in various shapes, sizes, and colors.

ANIMAL PARTS/BONES/FOSSILS

Ammonite Half

The ammonite fossil represents evolutional change and help activate the Kundalini. I use the traditional meaning of frequent change and progression.

Alligator Foot

In many cultures the alligator foot represents good luck. Because they walk on land and swim in water the natives used to think they started creation. Alligators were seen as signs of status and upper society. Traditionally, the alligator as a whole denotes holding onto something; therefore, I use the alligator foot to represent holding onto something while bringing good luck.

Alligator Scute

As a totem animal alligators are powerful, primal, and mighty animals on the planet. Spiritually, it means you should tap into your survival instincts. The alligator scute, to me, represents primal energies of survival.

Antelope Styrohyoid

Antelopes symbolize intelligence, wisdom, elegance, and grace; however, if seen in a dream, it is a

ANIMAL PARTS/BONES/FOSSILS

sign that your goals are hard to achieve and far away. I use this piece to represent intelligence and problems with achieving goals.

Armadillo Scale/Claw

Armadillos are covered with an armor-like covering of thick scales that protect them when being attacked. It even symbolizes protection and spiritual boundary. If you dream about an armadillo, it represents self-protection. The word "armadillo" literally means little armored one in the Spanish language. I use the armadillo scale/claw to mean armor, self-protection and resilience.

Badger Carpals

As a totem animal, badgers represent unconscious thoughts and aggression. They sometimes represent healing. Symbolically, when a badger appears in your life, you will never give up and always attain your goals. I have assigned the meaning of always attaining your goals along with never giving up on your projects to the badger carpals.

Bear Molar

Bears as a totem represent standing tall and strong. They are powerful and protective, especially of their offspring. They follow

ANIMAL PARTS/BONES/FOSSILS

and respect the rules. When I think of a bear, I think of the fact that they are known for hibernating in the winter. To me, the bear represents stepping back from a situation, especially to look at it from another perspective. It may mean to let someone else take charge or shine in the light, but the most important thing is to pull back and "hibernate".

Beaver Nail

Beavers are extremely hard-working little creatures. They literally symbolize being diligent and determined to finish their job when used as a totem animal. Beavers are very persistent. They are always digging and moving around creating their home and feeding their families. Therefore, the beaver nail represents busy, sometimes too busy depending on where it lands in reading.

Beaver Tooth

Beavers are extremely hard-working little creatures. They literally symbolize being diligent and determined to finish their job when used as a totem animal. As stated above, beavers are hard-working animals, determined to complete tasks. They represent hard work. I use the beaver tooth to represent this and to also represent needing to work harder or being overworked, depending on where it falls in the reading.

ANIMAL PARTS/BONES/FOSSILS

Black Widow Spider

Black widows symbolize independence. Black widows are commonly known for their sexual power and self-reliance. It may mean you are in a relationship that you do not want to be in and feel "trapped". I use the meaning of independence and sexual power (especially in the feminine essence).

Boar Tooth

The boar as a totem means someone who does not wait around for things to happen. He/She takes action. Symbolically, the boar signifies abundance, but can also represent conflict and disorder. Traditionally, it represents gaining success.

Bobcat Claw

The bobcat symbolizes lessons learned and balancing strategy with cheerfulness. If you dream of a bobcat, it usually means bad news is coming. I have chosen the bobcat claw to mean the bringing of bad news.

Bone Dice

- One dice is used for the following: Beginnings, Choices, Things flowing smoothly, Stability, Strife and conflict and Things coming

ANIMAL PARTS/BONES/FOSSILS

to highest point of development

- One dice is used for time frame of reading by weeks. You may use dice with as many sides as you wish in order to give more options for the timeframes for your readings.

- One dice may also be used to show the strength of surrounding pieces: One, it would be lesser bad news while six, would be really bad news.

Buffalo Bone Bead

This is a personal meaning. I needed a meaning for moderation and the bead resonated that with me.

Buffalo Bone Fish or Fish Curio

The traditional meaning of this piece is to dig deep down within yourself to figure out what the issue really is. Address it and you will be able to move on; dig deep and explore what has been kept hiding away; you will then be able to move on in this area freely.

Buffalo Bone Lion

As a totem, the lion dominates through strength. It imbues self-confidence. The lion spirituality symbolizes leadership. I assigned "Leader" to this piece for that reason.

ANIMAL PARTS/BONES/FOSSILS

Buffalo Bone Peace Sign

The peace sign originally stood for "nuclear disarmament" and was created from an "A" and a "D". It became popular in the United States for those protesting the Vietnam War. Today the Peace sign is generally used commonly for calmness and tranquility. The peace sign in the bones represents exactly what it stands for.

Buffalo Bone Pick

When reading, it is useful to have a piece that the Querent may use to point out pieces and groupings he/she may have questions about. This piece is long in nature, however not as long as the African porcupine pointer, so I feel it was perfect for this purpose.

Buffalo Tooth

Symbolically, the buffalo, due to their size, represents durability and firmness. It also exemplifies abundance and prosperity, while representing strength and stability. Traditionally, it represents abundance.

Carrion Crow Foot

In some cultures, the crow symbolizes good luck as in life,

ANIMAL PARTS/BONES/FOSSILS

intelligence, and magic. For most, a crow usually represents bad luck and misfortune. I modified the latter meaning to change it slightly by just bad luck to the piece that is touching the claw of the foot, as if stuck in its grasp.

Cat Foot

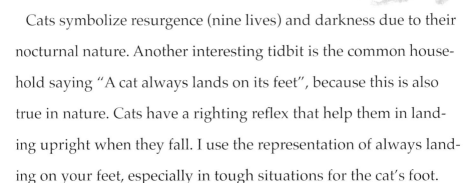

Cats symbolize resurgence (nine lives) and darkness due to their nocturnal nature. Another interesting tidbit is the common household saying "A cat always lands on its feet", because this is also true in nature. Cats have a righting reflex that help them in landing upright when they fall. I use the representation of always landing on your feet, especially in tough situations for the cat's foot.

Cat Neck Bone

The cat neck bone represents the "black cat" bone in readings. Black cats in England are considered good luck when given to a bride as a wedding present. Also, in Scotland, it is a sign of prosperity when a black cat shows up on your doorstep. The "black cat" neck bone is traditionally considered lucky when pointing to a piece.

Chicken Bone

Chickens are known to be dirty birds. Chicken coops must be

ANIMAL PARTS/BONES/FOSSILS

cleaned on a daily basis. Therefore, traditionally, one chicken bone represents the need to "clean out the coop or clean up the situation at hand. Also, chicken bones are popular being used as general bones that can take on many meanings when marked. (Samples given at the end of this section and explained more in chapter 6.)

Chicken Foot Bone

The chicken foot in hoodoo has very strong meaning of protection, luck, and good fortune, primarily when it comes to yourself. It also protects belongings, your home, and anything you own from being taken from you. Traditionally, the chicken foot is used for protection of the Querent's belongings and person.

Chipmunk Foot

Chipmunks symbolically represent prosperity, enjoyment, and playfulness. They are energetic and restless and quick. They are very resourceful little creatures. I use the middle literal meanings to create the chipmunk foot as energetic, restlessness, and speed.

Cougar Tooth

The spiritual meaning of the cougar is that you are very

ANIMAL PARTS/BONES/FOSSILS

protective, especially with the ones you love. Symbolically, the cougar is known to be a solitary animal – very graceful and powerful. I use the literal symbolic meanings for the cougar tooth to mean solidarity – gracefulness and powerful.

Cow Hide – Suede

The cow is a very useful animal with many useful parts, even down to the hide. Thus, this piece resonates with me usefulness due to its many purposes.

Coyote Knuckle – Small

Spiritually, when you see a coyote, you need to find balance between playfulness and wisdom. We use the small coyote knuckle to represent that. NOTE: If you have only one knuckle in your kit, it stands for both small and large knuckle meanings!

Coyote Knuckle – Large

In dreams, coyotes are known to be "tricksters" or "jokesters". We use the large coyote knuckle for that representation. NOTE: If you have only one knuckle in your kit, it stands for both small and large knuckle meanings!

ANIMAL PARTS/BONES/FOSSILS

Deer Molar

The tribes of North America view the deer as a gentle creature with intuitive instincts. It also represents a gentle and sensitive nature. Traditionally, the deer molar represents intuition and to trust your instincts.

Deer Antler Slice

The male deer is considered the guardian and protector of all of the other animals in the forest – the home. Traditionally, the deer antler slice represents home and hearth.

Deer Toe Bone

As a totem, the deer stands sturdy and strong, and is a peaceful creature. On the human, the function of the big toe along with the function of the little toe provides balance and stability when standing. I modified this and created the "stability" meaning in this way.

Dog – Furbaby Tooth

Dogs provide us with comfort and love in our lives, becoming part of our families. Puppies, or "furbabies" as we call them when they are young, lose baby teeth just as human

ANIMAL PARTS/BONES/FOSSILS

babies do. If you are lucky to find one, it may represent the comfort that these little precious ones give us. I assign comfort to the Querent for this piece.

Dog – Sacrum

Throughout history, dogs have always been known to be loyal, faithful, and protective. The sacrum is used for strength and stableness. For this reason, I combined the two and choose the dog sacrum to mean loyalty and protection.

Fish Bone – Small

Fish live in the water and go very deep as the weather gets cold. As our lives get hard, we have the feeling of being overwhelmed and life is overtaking us. To me, the fish represents not in the Querent's favor and "drowning" – in over his/her head.

Fish Bone – Large

The spirit animal fish denotes creativeness, deeper awareness, change, endurance, intelligence, health, and many more wonderful traits. Although the large fish bone may represent any of these qualities, I choose creativity, intelligence, and endurance.

ANIMAL PARTS/BONES/FOSSILS

Fox Bone

Foxes are able to escape tricky situations thru their cunningness. In literature, foxes are known to be sly, quiet, sneaky, and elusive creatures. Traditionally, the fox represents sly and sneakiness.

Fox (Silver) Fur, Ear, Nose

The fox spirit animal is known to be clever and shows great discernment, especially when someone is trying to deceive you. In this sense, the fox fur represents the ability to see through that and shows cleverness.

Fruit Bat Skull

The fruit bat, as a spirit totem animal, has many meanings including awareness of your surroundings and having psychic abilities. It can also represent the ending of bad habits. The meaning that most resonates with me is that the Querent has a perception of seeing things around him/her that others cannot.

Groundhog Claw

Groundhogs are family and community animals. They are known for loyalty, generosity, happiness, and hard work. For me, the groundhog claw represents generosity.

ANIMAL PARTS/BONES/FOSSILS

Horse Tail Bone

Animals use their tails to "sweep" away and clean the air and area behind them. Symbolically, the horse represents travel, desires, power, and freedom without restraint (www.universeofsymbolism.com). I used the literal meaning of freedom without restraint.

Horse Tooth

Once again, symbolically, the horse represents travel, desires, power, and freedom without restraint (www.universeofsymbolism.com). Traditionally, the horse tooth represents intuition.

Human Finger Tip

This is another example of where I needed a piece to represent a specific meaning. I felt the human fingertip helps create balance physiologically, so I feel the human fingertip creates a balance of responsibility in the Querent's life.

Human Phalange

The phalange is a vital part of the human hand. Because of this, I use the human phalange to mean the need to lend a helping hand

ANIMAL PARTS/BONES/FOSSILS

or the needing of help, depending on where it lands in the reading.

Human Tooth

Human teeth are essential parts of the human body. I use the tooth as the meaning of the Querent looking deep within to find answers to questions that he/she is facing.

Lamb Tooth

Symbolically, the lamb tooth represents chastity and virtue. It also represents gentleness. Traditionally, the lamb means you must make sacrifices. If by the lion piece, it means forgiveness.

Llama Bone

The llama symbolizes great strength and confidence. As a totem animal it represents communication and perseverance. I use the totem animal representation of perseverance for my meaning.

Lynx Bone

As a spirit animal, the lynx represents variety of meanings including secrets, revealing secrets, patience, passion, trust and many more. Although you may choose any of

ANIMAL PARTS/BONES/FOSSILS

the above, I choose revealing secrets for my meaning.

Mammoth Tusk Fossil

As a spirit animal, the mammoth represents ones physical traits; however, as a mystical creature, it represents a strong guardian, protector and something that provides guidance. I choose the meaning of a guardian, a protector and providing guidance.

Mink Bone

Minks have an acute sense of being adaptable and a sharp sense for intuition and timing. Traditionally, the mink represents adaptability to change.

Munia Bird Skull (Finch)

The finch represents and symbolizes enjoyment and enthusiasm of life. They are generally happy little creatures with a look of "brighter days on the horizon". They have high energy and enjoy every single day on this earth. To me, the finch skull represents enthusiasm of life.

Muskrat Mandible

Muskrat Teeth come attached to the jaw, which is vital in communicating with someone verbally. One side of the Muskrat's

ANIMAL PARTS/BONES/FOSSILS

Teeth is smooth, while the other side has a rough appearance. When the smooth side lands up in a reading, it represents good communication, while the rough side shows bad communication. Traditionally, two muskrat mandible jaws are used and only the smooth sides are speaking, one with three back dots. The one with the smooth side means good communication and the piece with three black dots represents bad communication.

Opossum Tooth

The opossum symbolizes in both life and dreams a person that does not care about being deceptive to get what they want. Their behavior is awful and they feel no remorse. Traditionally, the opossum stands for something that was hurt, damaged or broken and is now healed; therefore, that is what the opossum tooth represents.

Orthoceras Fossil

It is thought that the Orthoceras fossil brings balance to your emotions. It helps to stimulate your mind and increases confidence. I use the meaning of increases confidence.

Ostrich Toenail

Ostriches specifically symbolize great wealth and abundance;

ANIMAL PARTS/BONES/FOSSILS

therefore, I assign the meaning of great wealth and abundance in the future.

Otter Bone

Otters live in very social environments and are very social creatures. Their lives are consistently changing and moving. They are both symbolically earth and water elements. Traditionally the otter bone means transitions.

Owl Bone

In modern America, owls are known as creatures of great wisdom; therefore, an owl bone can tell us to be wise in making decisions about a situation. In other cultures, including ancient Native American lore, the owl is an omen of death. However, like the Tarot card, this is not necessarily literal. It can simply be the end of something or the beginning of something new. Because owls are the only known bird to be able to turn their heads almost completely around, I chose the bone to mean that the Querent is "seeing in all directions."

Owl Claw

Claws are used to grasp things tightly. The meaning

ANIMAL PARTS/BONES/FOSSILS

for the owl claw is to grasp tightly to someone or something.

Owl/Hawk Feather

Feathers of any kind are a symbol of flight and freedom. With the owl being such a strong creature in nature, I assigned this meaning to the owl feather, both literally and figuratively.

Pheasant Neck Bone

The pheasant spirit animal taps into raw power, usually sexual in nature, to accomplish creative goals and achieve success; thus, to me, being creative and producing accomplishments by tapping into passions and talents.

Pig Rib Bone

Pigs symbolize great wealth and money as well as luck. When most people think of pigs, we think of gluttony, overeating, or over doing something. The saying "Pig Out" comes from this widespread attitude. From this, we get the meanings of gluttony; and too much of something pertaining to the piece it is near.

Porcupine Carpal

When seeing porcupines in dreams, you might want to be careful that obstacles or situations of trouble and misunderstand-

ANIMAL PARTS/BONES/FOSSILS

ings might occur. Traditionally, the porcupine represents a situation to be cautious and wise.

Porcupine Quill – African

The African Porcupine Quill is very and traditionally is used by the reader for a pointer during the reading so as not to touch the bones with one's hands.

Porcupine Quill – American

When seeing porcupines in dreams, you might want to be careful that obstacles or situations of trouble and misunderstandings might occur. Traditionally, the porcupine represents a situation to be cautious and wise. They also may be used as pointers and dividers, but are very sharp. I assign the meaning "strike hard and fast" to the quills as the porcupine is not an animal to mess with!

Rabbit Mandible

Rabbits symbolize endurance. Their act of multiplying quickly gives them a spirit meaning of fertility. Abundance and prosperity are two other symbolic meanings of the rabbit. I use the rabbit to symbolize fertility and prosperity.

ANIMAL PARTS/BONES/FOSSILS

Raccoon Baculum

In the American South, a popular hoodoo charm is the Raccoon Baculum. It is said that carrying the bone can bring luck, especially in finances, yet some are said to use it as an aphrodisiac or fertility charm. To me, they both ring true in a sense, giving the meaning of being lucky in love with fidelity and having a good person who will care for you. Traditionally, the baculum represents fidelity and love.

Raccoon Bone

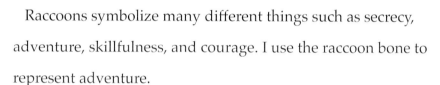

Raccoons symbolize many different things such as secrecy, adventure, skillfulness, and courage. I use the raccoon bone to represent adventure.

Rat Bones

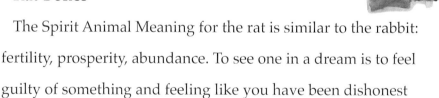

The Spirit Animal Meaning for the rat is similar to the rabbit: fertility, prosperity, abundance. To see one in a dream is to feel guilty of something and feeling like you have been dishonest regarding something. Traditionally, the rat means adaptability.

Rattlesnake/Cobra Ribs

When you think of snakes, you think of constricting. Also,

ANIMAL PARTS/BONES/FOSSILS

transformations come to mind, which is what they represent. The ribs of the snake are commonly used for dividers. If only one is used, it traditionally stands for constriction.

Saber Toothed Herring Fossil

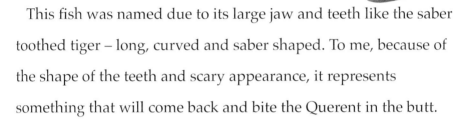

This fish was named due to its large jaw and teeth like the saber toothed tiger – long, curved and saber shaped. To me, because of the shape of the teeth and scary appearance, it represents something that will come back and bite the Querent in the butt.

Scorpion

The scorpion is a ferocious and wild creature with an astounding defense mechanism. Spiritually, it represents passion and new love. I use the scorpion to mean defense and passion.

Shark Tooth

When we think of the shark, we think of blood, danger, and fear. Traditionally, this piece means beware, a warning out for blood.

Snake Vertebrae

Snakes are flexible, yet strong and can climb walls almost to their full length. Traditionally, snake vertebrae stands for

ANIMAL PARTS/BONES/FOSSILS

flexibility, backbone, strength, and standing tall.

Snakeskin Shed

Snakes generally represent transitions and transformations. They also represent constriction. Snake skin shed is traditionally used for meaning transformations.

Squirrel Claw

Squirrels represent many things like being social, happiness, and being focused. Squirrels are known to hide acorns for food for later. I use the squirrel claw to represent saving up now for future times of need.

Stingray Barb

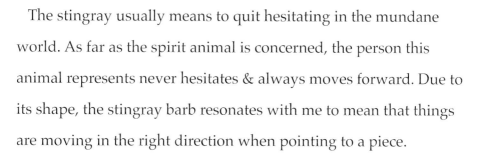

The stingray usually means to quit hesitating in the mundane world. As far as the spirit animal is concerned, the person this animal represents never hesitates & always moves forward. Due to its shape, the stingray barb resonates with me to mean that things are moving in the right direction when pointing to a piece.

Turkey Bone or Wish Bone

In the mundane world, the turkey means you need more balance.

ANIMAL PARTS/BONES/FOSSILS

As far as dream interpretation, it means you need to do what is right and true. Traditionally, it means unlocking potential.

Turtle Bone

The turtle represents patience, fertility, and good fortune. To me, it means the Querent needs to come out of his/her shell and step into the light – step out of the shadows.

Turtle Shell

The turtle represents patience, fertility, and good fortune. I use the shell to mean that something is hiding from the Querent – as if hidden under the shell.

Viper Fangs

Thinking of viper snakes, what comes to mind is dangerous circumstances or to "strike". To me, a warning of an attack appropriately fits this piece.

Walrus Tooth Fossil

Walruses are kind, loving, and social animals. The traditional meaning of a walrus is someone who obeys rules and agrees with others easily – too easily.

ANIMAL PARTS/BONES/FOSSILS

Whale Vertebrae Fossil

People usually relate whales to mean your inner voice. Other associations include communication and awareness. Because of a whale's size, the whale bone fossil resonates with me a huge event happening in the future, depending on the number of weeks the dice represents; therefore, that is what I use it for.

Wolf Hair

The symbolism of the wolf brings to you that you can work well with others in a "pack", so to say. It also means to trust your instincts more if it represents you as a spirit animal. When thinking of wolves, protection comes to mind. The wolf hair, to me, represents that the Querent must work in a group.

Woodpecker Bone

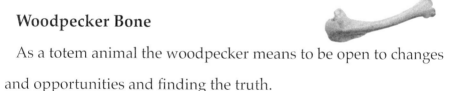

As a totem animal the woodpecker means to be open to changes and opportunities and finding the truth.

Woodpecker Foot

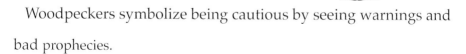

Woodpeckers symbolize being cautious by seeing warnings and bad prophecies.

ANIMAL PARTS/BONES/FOSSILS

MISCELLANEOUS BONE MEANINGS

PERSONAL

Sometimes you need a piece to represent something you do not have in your set. Or, you may have an excess amount of animal bones around that you could put to use. It is perfectly acceptable to use excess animal bones (i.e. turkey, chicken, fish…) for this purpose. I sometimes label mine and then assign meanings OR just simply assign a meaning. Notice below I give my bones labels. You do not have to do this. I just do it for my own preference. Some examples are as follows:

Fish Bone w/Hole

I needed a piece to represent a subject (Legal Matters) and used a miscellaneous bone to do so. (As with chicken bones, fish bones are great to use as miscellaneous bones for personal pieces.)

Miscellaneous Bone (fish bone I found on the beach)

I needed a piece to represent a subject (Family) and used a miscellaneous bone to do so. I found this one on the beach during a family vacation; therefore, it was a perfect fit.

ANIMAL PARTS/BONES/FOSSILS

Sun Deer Flange

The sun represents power and strength.

Water Chicken Bone

Water represents reconciliation, healing, fixing.

Earth Chicken Bone

Security of something – needed a piece for this

Mars Chicken Bone

Battle and conflict – needed a piece for this

Mercury Chicken Bone

Bad habits overcoming – needed a piece for this

Moon Chicken Bone

Psychic energies – needed a piece for this

Universe Chicken Bone

The whole world is at your fingertips! – needed a piece for this (I got this name idea from the Tarot deck.)

ANIMAL PARTS/BONES/FOSSILS

Air Chicken Bone

Wishes - needed a piece for this

Fire Chicken Bone

Passion - needed a piece for this

Spirit Chicken Bone

Connecting with the divine - needed a piece for this

Truth Chicken Bone

Truth - needed a piece for this

CERAMIC/CLAY/GLASS/PORCELAIN

Doll Arm

Looking at an extended out hand reminds us of either giving or receiving. Traditionally, the doll arm, if up, represents that the Querent is giving too much; and, if down, the Querent is in need.

Doll Face

Traditionally, the doll face means Spirit Guide is watching the Querent in this area.

Bottle/Message Bottle

Messages are written on paper and put in bottles and have been for centuries to cast out in the ocean for strangers to find. I assign the bottle/message bottle to mean a message was coming to the Querent regarding the surrounding pieces.

Marble

When we think of marbles we think of children playing. Traditionally, the marble represents playfulness.

CERAMIC/CLAY/GLASS/PORCELAIN

Pottery Shard

The pottery shard is an ancient piece of history. It is good to have a very old piece in your collection that connects you to your Ancestors. This is a way to communicate with your Ancestors for guidance during the reading.

Spiral

Spirals can represent the beginning and the end. Also, they represent the beginning of a long journey as well as moving in a particular direction. Ancient Celts viewed it as the transformation through life. To me, the spiral represents a new beginning.

Thimble

In ancient times, a man would give a thimble to a woman of whom he wanted to court. Thimbles are used throughout history to protect the fingers of a person who is sewing. There are so many uses for the thimble. Traditionally, the thimble means work and/or school.

GEMS/STONE

Amethyst

Amethyst gets rid of negative connotations and provides a shield against unwanted energies. It promotes peace, calmness, and spiritual healing. It helps both spiritually and physically. I choose the amethyst to represent calm; helping with physical and emotional problems.

Arrowhead

We tend to think Native American culture when we think of an arrowhead. Among other meanings, the arrow in their culture mainly symbolizes protection. In our society the arrow usually means direction and shows movement. Because I think of Native American Culture, I use the definition of protection.

Citrine

By their color alone citrine remind us of beautiful sunny days, warm fuzzy feelings, and bright happiness. Citrine, most often, represents being in good health and having great success.

Corporlite

Corporlite traditionally represents something that no longer serves us like issues or behaviors.

GEMS/STONES

Crystal – Tibetan

Tibetan crystals are of bad clarity and "muddy" in appearance. To me, they show that the Querent is in an unclear, muddy situation. Most Tibetan crystals are a muddy color. However, any crystal will do here.

Dessert Rose

The desert rose, in the mundane world, is all about energy and processing information. It helps you to get out of a rut. That is what it represents to me.

Emerald

The emerald is usually connected to the heart chakra, providing unconditional love and concern for suffering. Green is usually associated with money. I choose the emerald for its color meaning of cash coming the Querent's way.

Fluorite

Fluorite is connected to the upper chakras. It links the mind to universal collective consciousness.

Goddess Stone

A round shaped stone that reminded me of the Goddess is what I

GEMS/STONE

use to represent this subject.

Hag Stone

The hag stone is traditionally used in magic to see the truth; therefore, the hag stone represents seeing the truth.

Hematite Bracelet – (Any Gemstone Bracelet Will Do)

The hematite bracelet traditionally means to look over here and that what is enclosed is very important to the reading.

Herkimer Diamond

Herkimer Diamonds are well known for cleansing and purifying. Traditionally, the Herkimer Diamond is a piece that calls for you to "look over here" because this is important.

Howlite Pick

Howlite connects the spirit with energies of the universe. I think it is appropriate to be used by the Questioner when pointing out pieces or clusters that they are attracted to, as it is better and seen as more respectful to not physically touch the pieces.

GEMS/STONES

Howlite Skull

To the norm, the skull is associated with death and mortality. That is probably why traditionally it represents the Ancestors and if they are in your favor. If the skull is facing outward, it means they are not happy with the Querent and the need to work with them. If facing inward, they are blessing the Querent.

Pearl – Freshwater

The pearl represents purity and virtue. It is also known to symbolize generosity, loyalty, and strengthen relationships. I choose the pearl to represent purity and freedom from contamination.

Rose Quartz

Rose quartz universally means love and romance. The traditional meaning of this piece is happiness.

Ruby

Rubies have been utilized for hundreds of years for many different applications including passion, love, healing and power. The color itself represents love in many cultures. I use the ruby to represent passionate love.

GEMS/STONE

Selenite

Selenite has many magical uses. Some include clearing negative energy, clearing the mind of clutter, and promoting calmness. I use selenite to represent clearing the mind and dispelling negative energy.

Stone of Choice

You will need a stone that is flat on one side and rough on the other. It does not matter the type of stone. If the smooth side is up, things are running smoothly. If the rough side is up, things are a little on the "rocky" side.

Tawny Agate

Tawny agate was used centuries ago for luck in battle. Today, It is still used, but for power of a situation. It was also used to ward off the evil eye. The stone promotes energy. I use the stone to represent energy.

HERBS/NUTS/SEEDS/ROOTS

Buckeye Nut

In most cultures, the buckeye nut means good luck. Traditionally, it symbolizes health. If the eye side is up, it means bad health. If the eye side is down, it means good health. I use the traditional meaning; however, I also use it for the "Health" of a subject piece if it falls next to one.

High John the Conqueror Root

Typically, High John is used for many different things In Hoodoo. Those include sex spells, good luck mojo bags, and protection. I use this root to represent male influences and energies.

Lavender

Lavender is known worldwide for its calming effect and promoting sleep. I use lavender to represent calmness.

Moonflower Seed

Moonflowers only bloom in the night and dark skies. I use it to represent something good is coming out of a dark situation.

HERBS/NUTS/SEEDS/ROOTS

Nutmeg

Magically, nutmeg is used for luck, prosperity, money and health. I use nutmeg to represent good luck.

Vanilla Beans

Magically, vanilla is used for love and is one of the most popular oils used in magic. Symbolically, it represents purity, innocence, and comfort. Traditionally, vanilla beans in whole are used for dividers and pointers.

METAL

Angel

Angels represent love, truth, and faith. To some people, angels are guardians sent to watch over people. Angelic magic is used to create and destroy. I use the angel to represent the Guardian Angel.

Arrow

Arrows bring to mind direction and movement. They can also represent power and moving ahead in life without regret, always looking forward and not living in the past. Traditionally, the arrow represents something moving quickly.

Bat

Bats are good at seeing things in the dark that others cannot due to their physical attributes. When people think of bats, they think of the dark. Symbolically, bats represent concluding projects and beginning new ones. Years ago, bats were used in formulas to cure ailments and conditions. I use the bat to represent the dark side of a situation.

Bell

Bells are used for many things including clearing energy. Traditionally, the bell represents happiness.

METAL

Button

Buttons of different materials have individual meanings. For example, a button made of material represents a person's health is deteriorating. Buttons in general stand for a possible trip in the future. Traditionally, buttons are used in a reading for "connecting".

Cameo

Cameos were originally used to represent important events. Symbolically, they attract good health and fortune, which is what I use them for.

Coffin nail

Coffin nails can be used to break a curse as well as put power into a curse. Traditionally, the coffin nail represents the end of something or death of something.

Coin

Coins represent good luck as well as prosperity. Traditionally, the coin represents money and finances.

Copper Nugget

Copper is used for cleansing and healing. It also influences

METAL

energy. Traditionally, copper means that there is healing in progress.

Crucifix

Throughout history, the crucifix has mainly stood for when Christ was crucified. This way of punishment was kept for the most severe of crimes. The crucifix is the main symbol of Christianity. Traditionally, it represents sacrifices if facing up and blessings will come if facing down.

Elephant Charm

Elephants have an amazing memory and are known for that. In some cultures they are known to bring good luck. In Buddhism, the elephant represents the beginning of a figurative journey. I use the meaning of memory. The elephant represents remembering something from the Querent's past to help in the present or future situation.

Fish Hook

The fish hook is another piece that represents good luck. In Hawaii it represents your connection to the water. Traditionally, the fish hook represents something that is holding the Querent back.

METAL

Fishing Weight

Weights in general represent a measure of substantial mass. Emotionally, they represent something that is "weighing" heavy on your shoulders and bring you down. Traditionally, the fishing weight represents the emotional meaning of "weighing" heavy on the Querent's shoulders and bringing him/her down.

Frame w/Courage Photo

I needed a piece to represent courage and found this little frame with a picture of an angel in it and the word "Courage" written on it.

Handcuffs

When you see handcuffs you think of jail and being locked up. Handcuffs also represent being restrained. Traditionally, the handcuffs represent the need to get rid of something in the Querent's life that no longer serves for good and is destructive.

Heart w/Leather Straps

The heart represents love in most cultures. Leather is commonly used to tie things down when needed. The combination of the

METAL

heart with the leather wrapped around it worked perfectly for what I needed, which was a piece to represent something/someone that holds the Querent down in a relationship.

Key

In some cultures keys represent opening doors between worlds, while in others it represents opening doors to new opportunities. Traditionally, the key represents opportunities.

Lock

Locks can have different meanings depending on whether they are opened or closed. For example, a closed lock without a key can represent love everlasting or being locked into a situation. I use the lock to represent being trapped in certain circumstances or with a particular person.

Ring

Rings, being circular, can represent the circle of life. The spiritual meaning of the ring draws divinity to whomever wears it. Traditionally, as to most, the ring represents commitment.

Safety Pin

The safety pin is the same as a regular pin, but has an enclosed

METAL

piece to fasten the sharp end to form a loop and keep the sharp end covered and therefore "safe". The traditional meaning of the safety pin is to be safe in this area (pieces surrounding or near this pin).

Skeleton

The symbolic meaning of the skeleton is finding truth. The saying of "skeletons in your closet" is very common to most. I use the skeleton to mean the Querent or someone near the Querent has skeletons in their closet that may be brought to the surface.

Thimble

In ancient times, a man would give a thimble to a woman of whom he wanted to court. Thimbles are used throughout history to protect the fingers of a person who is sewing. There are so many uses for the thimble. Traditionally, the thimble means work and/or school.

Triple Goddess

The Triple Goddess can represent all three phases of the moon – maiden, mother, and crone – waxing, full, and waning. The Goddess is a Deity that comes in many forms,

METAL

sometimes all three as Hecate is. I use the Triple Goddess to represent a Deity that may or may not watch over the Querent, depending on where it lands.

Turtle

The turtle symbolically represents endurance and good health. When most people think of the turtle, they think of things moving slowly. I use the meaning of things moving slowly regarding the pieces surrounding it.

Viking Pick

Vikings are known to be violent and brutal warriors. I use the Viking Pick to mean that a fight or an argument may come to the Querent.

PLASTIC/WOOD/OTHER

Bamboo

Bamboo is considered lucky and brings unity in one's life. Other meanings include flexibility and strength. I use bamboo to mean balance in whichever piece it falls by.

Beads

Beads are traditionally used to represent the Querent and other people for the reading.

Cork

Corks, in a magical sense, are good luck. Corking is sometimes used for insulation. They are also used to plug bottles of wine. I use the cork to mean "stop".

Button

Buttons are used for fastening and fixing material and other things together. The traditional meaning for a button is "connecting" two pieces or more together.

Dice

- Dice are used for time framings in weeks and months.
- Traditionally, one dice is used for the following:

PLASTIC/WOOD/OTHER

1 – Beginnings

2 – Choices

3 – Things flowing smoothly

4 – Stability

5 – Strife and conflict

6 – Things coming to highest point of development

- One dice may also be used to show the strength of surrounding pieces. For example, if the dice landed next to the bad news piece and is a 6, it would mean really bad news. If it was a 1, it would be lesser bad news.

Domino

Dominoes commonly represent loss and other failures. Traditionally, if the numbers side is up, Querent is aware of circumstances. However, if the numbers side is down, Querent is not aware and in denial.

Frog

Because of their cycle of transitions, frogs mainly represent transformations. As a spirit animal, it means you need to go right into a tough situation and figure things out. Being a power animal, it gives you the power to figure out what the issue is and take care of it. I use the traditional meaning (also listed above), that the

PLASTIC/WOOD/OTHER

Querent will go through some transformations rather quickly.

Flower

Common meanings of the flower are hope, love, and beauty. I take the flower as bringing things to fruition. The result of hard work and great effort.

Lily Pads/Connected Discs

Because of the stair-step look of the lily pads, I choose the flat connected lily pads to represent stepping stones of a situation or project. (Also listed in gems and stones)

Wasp Nest

Wasps work well as a community so I choose this piece to represent the Querent works well with others and with a community.

Worry Dolls

I use the worry dolls to represent the Querent and other people during a reading. This works especially for when doing events and multiple readings in a row. The Querent may take them home and use the worry dolls and even bring them back for future readings.

SHELLS

In bone reading, shells are used to represent many different things. Some shells have a traditional meaning, while most meanings are assigned by the Reader. I listed my assignments to shells and the traditional meanings when applicable.

Abalone Shell – Flat

Traditional meaning of helpful talents will come out here.

Abalone Shell – Swirl

My starter piece.

Beehive Shell

Current or future projects referring to what pieces it is by.

Cat's Eye Shell

Traditionally, if the eye side is up, Querent is seeing things clearly. If the eye side is down, Querent is not seeing things clearly.

Center Cut Shell

This is a very feminine shaped shell so I assign it to mean female energies and influences such as empathy and nurturing qualities.

SHELLS

Conch Shell – Small

Traditionally, it means a pregnancy or something new.

Coral

Traditionally represents wisdom.

Cowrie Shells – Enclosed

Traditionally, these are used for "yes" and "no" questions. After thrown, if slit sides land up on both, the answer is yes. If the round sides land up, the answer is no. If one of each land, the answer is neither yes nor no. You must reword the question.

Cowrie Shell(s) – Open

If it lands upright, all surrounding pieces' meanings are opposite in this section of reading (just pieces in the cluster of which it lands or pieces directly touching or around the shell).

Elephant Tusk Shell

Loyalty, Strength (as elephants are known to be).

SHELLS

Heliacus Shell

Patience

Miscellaneous Shells

Traditionally, miscellaneous shells are used to represent people in readings. They are also used to assign meanings to when you do not have a piece to represent something.

Mother of Pearl Bird or Butterfly

Traditionally, the bird represents travel or journey both figuratively and literally.

Mother of Pearl Piece

Traditionally, mother of pearl represents spiritual work being helpful to the Querent.

Olive Shell

Traditionally, this shell represents things are running smoothly if the smooth side lands up.

Ram Horn Shell

As rams represent symbolically, this piece represents stubbornness.

SHELLS

Sand Dollar

If the sand dollar lands near coin, the money situation is good. If it lands far from the coin, there may be some financial struggles.

Seahorse

As the seahorse represents symbolically, this piece stands for strength and power.

Sea Urchin – Points

Traditionally, the pointed sea urchin pieces are used as pointers and dividers.

Sea Urchin – Round

As sea urchins represent symbolically obstacles, so does the sea urchin piece.

Starfish

Traditionally, starfish represent the Querent's need for spiritual work and growth.

SHELLS

Sundial Shell

As a sundial symbolizes brevity and shortness of time, so does the sundial shell.

TOOLS

Shells, Beads, Worry Dolls

Items to represent Querent

Anointing Oil

Used to bless Querent

African Porcupine Quill

Reader uses to point out pieces in reading

Bag

Holds your set and used to throw them

Basket or Bowl

Holds your set and used to throw them

Box

Holds your set and used to throw them

Candle & Holder

For connecting with Spirits and Spirit Guides

TOOLS

Florida Water, Hoyt's Cologne, Rose Water

Cleans your set

Frankincense and Myrrh Oils

Put a few drops in cleansing waters/colognes above to clean and feed bones thoroughly

Incense & Holder

Pays respect and attracts Spirit Guides and Ancestors

Lighter

To light candles, incense, sage…

Miscellaneous Items to Draw In Ancestors

Photos, articles of clothing, anything to help attract Ancestors

Offering Bowl/Plate/Glass

Bowl is used for water to attract Spirits and Ancestors and for clarity in reading – Plate is used to hold offerings to Deities, Spirits, Ancestors, and so forth – Glass is used for liquid offerings

TOOLS

Sage

To cleanse the reading space and area – also used for deep cleaning of your set periodically

Rattles, Drums, Bells

Used to create energy during beginning of reading

Throwing Mat

Place to throw the bones, shells, & curios for the reading – may also use another mat to place between throwing surface and mat for better connection to the earth (made of natural material)

GETTING STARTED & GENERAL INFORMATION

Everyone has their own individual method of reading bones; however, when first learning, you should keep the reading simple. As you get comfortable with yourself and gain confidence, you can graduate to more difficult reading styles. The following is my "Beginner Bone Reading" instruction.

Items you MUST have include:

A bone set (at least 18 pieces to start)

GETTING STARTED & GENERAL INFORMATION

A box or bag (to hold and store the bones)

An abalone shell, basket, or throwing bowl (used for casting if storing bones in a bag)

GETTING STARTED & GENERAL INFORMATION

A throwing mat or surface (place to throw bones during the reading)

Florida Water, Hoyt's Cologne, Rose Water, or sage (to cleanse between readings)

GETTING STARTED & GENERAL INFORMATION

Beads, shells, worry Dolls, or curio (to represent Querent during reading)

An African Porcupine quill or buffalo pick (to point to bones during a reading)

GETTING STARTED & GENERAL INFORMATION

An Ancestral Altar (to respectfully store bones on or when they are not in use)

Stryx celebrating Samhain with the Ancestors at Dragon Hill, TN

2-4 Cowrie Shells (to give yes/no answers during reading)

GETTING STARTED & GENERAL INFORMATION

Though they are not necessary, other items you may want to use are incense and/or anointed candles with holders to open the area and welcome the Ancestors and Spirit Guides. A glass or bowl of water may help to open up to the Spirits and help clarify your reading. We should always remember to thank the Ancestors, so an offering plate for gifts such as tobacco, mugwort, or whiskey is highly recommended. Bells, rattles, or drums can all raise energy and "wake up" the Ancestors while the Querent is concentrating and mixing the bones. To bless the Querent after the reading, which is called the "Crowning", anointing oil may be applied to the Querent's forehead. Any other items that you find that will help you personally tune in to your Ancestors are encouraged during readings.

Your container, which stores your bones, should be enclosed. Usually, you can throw them directly from this container; however, if you store them in a bag, you will need a bowl or basket as a "throwing" container. A flat basket, bowl, or abalone shell works nicely for this. You can easily throw them with your hands as well.

When choosing a mat or surface, choose one that calls to you. You can have multiple mats for the different types of readings. If you purchase one, chances are that it will either have the circle

GETTING STARTED & GENERAL INFORMATION

within a circle marking or the cross within a circle marking, as they are the most popular. If you make your own, you can put your own markings on it and personalize it to your liking. You may use any type of material, but natural fabrics, such as animal hide, are best. You may also want to use a throwing tray to prevent pieces from falling off your throwing mat. When first starting out, a simple piece of cloth or material is most useful. Some Readers place a fiber mat between the throwing mat and the throwing surface. This is done to help connect with the land.

When you get your bones, it is customary to clean and then set on your Ancestral Altar for a few days. Burn Frankincense and Myrrh to help connect with the spirits. You may also want to lightly put some on the bones by rubbing the oil in your hands and mixing them. Soaking in Florida Water, Rose Water, or Hoyt's Cologne is also a popular way to help clean and charge them right away. Below, we will discuss feeding and cleaning bones further.

Cleaning and consecrating your bones is the first step when either getting a new set or adding a new piece. It can be as simple as smudging with sage or sprinkling with salt, or it can involve performing a full ritual or ceremony in order to bless your pieces with each of the elements.

GETTING STARTED & GENERAL INFORMATION

You must then introduce your piece(s) to your Ancestors, Deities, and Spirit Guides. Introduce each piece separately, speaking aloud the name and meaning of the piece. Continue the process until all pieces are spoken, then close with asking for guidance, interpretation, and foresight. A small ritual is a great way to do this.

It is important to clean your bones in between every reading. You may do so by dusting with sage powder or lightly spraying with Florida Water, Hoyt's Cologne, or Rose Water. Always clean your bones immediately before the reading and not after. Putting your bones away damp may cause damage and mildew.

After multiple readings, you should clean your bones to rid them of residual energy by using the methods above. Feeding and cleaning your bones thoroughly and periodically shows respect to them and your Ancestors. You may do so by adding a pinch of mugwort, tobacco, or another herb that resonates with you to them in their container. Placing them on your Ancestral Alter for a few days and praying over them is another great way to clean them. You may also "smoke" them with sage or palo santo. After "smoking" them, put the soot with the bones in a container and lightly shake to feed them. A pinch of salt is always a good way to

GETTING STARTED & GENERAL INFORMATION

feed and clean bones. Also, you may add Frankincense and Myrrh to the cleansing waters to feed them. Of course, cleansing and charging them under the full moon is highly recommended.

In the beginning, it is important to bond with your bones. When you first get your set of bones or a new piece to add to your set, keep them close to you to form a relationship with them. Always try to carry them with you when possible. You can even place them under your pillow while sleeping. This will help you connect with them. When your bones are not with you, it is best to always store bones on or next to Ancestral Altar.

Introducing your bones to the Ancestors, Deities, and Spirit Guides is a start to memorizing your kit, then full memorization may begin during the bonding period, but it may take some time. I know this might seem a bit overwhelming in the beginning. Keep in mind it is not necessary to have your bones memorized before learning the basic reading technique. If you break it down and memorize the basic pieces first, then add 2-3 pieces each week, you will know your set in no time! A common mistake is trying to learn all the pieces at once. Take your time, holding each piece and speaking out loud what its meaning is, therefore connecting with it. It only takes a few minutes to do this, and if this is done

GETTING STARTED & GENERAL INFORMATION

on a nightly basis, it carries excellent results. It is important that you direct your voice to the Ancestors. Keep in mind, at first, you will be depending on the literal meanings of the bones. With experience, you will learn to use both literal and intuitive meanings to guide your reading.

As stated earlier in the book, the most common subjects are as follows:

Self (Querent)	Family (As a whole)	Friends (As a whole)
Children (As a whole)	Health	Work (If applicable)
School (If applicable)	Home and Hearth	Finances
Love and Romance	Travel	Projects and Activities
Legal Matters	Spirit Guides	Ancestors

You may include other subjects as you wish. Just be sure to have a piece to represent each one. Miscellaneous shells, beads, and chicken bones are excellent for this purpose, but curios are perfectly acceptable.

What happens when a piece gets lost or broken? When a piece gets lost, you have to make the decision of whether or not to "release" it by acknowledging to the Ancestors and Spirit Guides that it is gone. If it comes back to you, it may be used again. For

GETTING STARTED & GENERAL INFORMATION

example, I had a beehive shell that disappeared out of my collection. I looked through my basket multiple times and could not find it. A few days and many readings later, I found it exactly where I remembered it to be – in the basket I stored it in! It came back to me!

When a piece breaks or you are no longer using it, you may want to "retire" it. You must show it respect by burying it and thanking it for its service. You might even want to perform a small ceremony. At this time, it is considered "finished". For example, I retired a seahorse charm when I acquired a real seahorse. I buried the charm with thanks and gratitude and went on to use the new piece!

Know that it is perfectly acceptable to "gift" pieces you no longer use to others. The important thing to remember is that you must release it and they must clean the bone and present it to their Ancestors and such as it is a new piece in their collection.

PERSONALIZING YOUR SET

At this point, we look at one of the best parts of reading bones – creating your bone set! Keep in mind that no two bone sets are the same, and no two meaning sets are the same. Once you start expanding your collection and assigning personal meanings to some of the pieces, your set becomes your own unique collection.

There are a few ways to create and expand your set. You can purchase a starter or deluxe set and go from there. Look at the most common subjects and be sure to have a piece representing each one. This is why you want to expand. Adding to your collection also gives you information for a more detailed reading.

After acquiring your original set, you may purchase supplementary sets, purchase bones from metaphysical stores, or purchase bones from online stores. The downside to purchasing online is that you may have to purchase in small bulk and end up with multiples. Purchasing online can also be more expensive. To add to your set, you may also find and use roadkill or hunted animals. Pieces can be randomly found as well. For example, I found a beautiful bone on the beach during a family vacation, which is now my Family piece. Remember, curios such as charms from jewelry and other trinkets are also "pieces" and can be

PERSONALIZING YOUR SET

found. It's also acceptable to use bones from the food you eat.

Note that there is no limit to the number of pieces a bone collection can have. The more you have, the more detailed the reading is.

A fun way to expand your collection is to find other bone enthusiasts and trade off duplicate pieces. As mentioned above, when buying from online shops or stores, you end up with extra pieces most of the time. Use these extras to trade for other pieces you might need or want. Be sure, no matter where you get them, the bones were collected "cruelty free" and no harm was done to the animals.

If you decide to use bones from roadkill or food that you eat to expand your set, you must know how to clean the bones properly. Even so, be aware of roadkill. You cannot guarantee the animal is

PERSONALIZING YOUR SET

disease free or what bacteria may be on the body. Preparation of your own bones is discussed in Chapter 7.

Remember two very important things- NEVER kill an animal just for its bones and ALWAYS thank the animal spirit for its sacrifice!!!

Collecting here and there is a fun way to expand your set and make it your very own. You may want to include pieces that are personal and have special meaning to you, such as pendants or charms. Collecting shells along the beach is also a great way to acquire pieces, along with using unique beads and curios you may come across.

As mentioned earlier, if a piece speaks to you, use it. If it already has a particular meaning assigned to it, but you intuitively feel it represents something else, go with your intuition.

You can always find meanings by researching what the animal, bone, or curio represents from existing books or internet searches of spiritual representations or symbolism. Keep in mind that each piece, especially bones, gives off a certain energy connected to it. I personally use traditional meanings first, while only assigning personal meanings when I cannot find the traditional one after

PERSONALIZING YOUR SET

research. You may find that you have multiple shells or multiple bones of a particular animal. You can mark these to represent anything you want. Just be sure, as with all of your bones, to introduce them to the Ancestors, Deities, and Spirit Guides for what they are and what they mean.

For example, I have five chicken bones that represent the following:

Moon	Psychic Energies
Sun	Power
Mercury	Breaking Bad Habits
Mars	Conflict

I also have seashells to represent personal meanings:

Beehive shell	Current or future projects
Sundial shell	Brevity; shortness of time
Ram shell	Stubbornness
Heliacus shell	Patience
Miscellaneous shell	Family

PERSONALIZING YOUR SET

I use candle color representations when assigning meanings to multiple colored items such as feathers.

I have some bones that I could not find meanings for, so I looked the animal up on the internet to see what it represented. One example is the armadillo. I have an armadillo scale, and since the armadillo represents protection, that is what I assigned as the meaning. Another example is the rabbit. The rabbit represents fertility and prosperity, so my rabbit mandible represents that in my collection.

If a piece is fragile, you might want to lightly coat it in acrylic to make it firm. There are some people who oppose this solution, as they believe all pieces should be natural, but it is commonly accepted for most.

Keep in mind that you may also want a small set of bones for travel. This set may consist of only approximately twenty-five pieces or so and just give basic, general information. Unfortunately, you cannot have all of your subject pieces in your travel set. You may only want to include Querent, finances, love and romance, and an extra shell to represent a subject of the Querent's choice.

PREPARATION OF FRESH BONES AND FEET

When dealing with roadkill or other found animals, it is important to take into consideration how they died, what kind of life they lived, and what conditions they died under. For example, if an animal dies a brutal death, the bones might give off a negative energy. In any case, you must clean the residual energies from the bones before even processing them. You may do so with something as simple as "smoking" them with sage. I prefer to do a full ritual to clean them of all unwanted energy.

Cleaning and Preparing Bones:

I learned this method of cleaning bones from multiple websites and seasoned practitioners. This method of cleaning bones is basic and may not be used for more complicated bones such as skulls or large wings. It is possible, but difficult.

1. To clean fresh bones, be sure to start with removing all flesh and cartilage. If you leave anything on the bones, it will cause complications later.

2. Next, boil bones to remove all remaining flesh. This will take approximately four hours. Do not use a rolling boil. A hard simmer works best. Let cool completely. Instead of using the

PREPARATION OF FRESH BONES AND FEET

previous method, you may also cook them on high in a slow cooker at 165 degrees for twenty-four hours.

3. Finish cleaning off all meat and cartilage by hand.

4. Soak in lightly diluted Dawn dish liquid for at least twelve hours. This removes all grease and residue.

5. After removing all grease, soak in 3% hydrogen peroxide until the bones are a desired shade of white. You may use hydrogen peroxide from any drugstore for this step.

6. Thoroughly rinse and dry.

7. Paint if desired.

Note: You may also want to set them in the sun for a few hours to whiten them further, but do this with precaution. Be sure to check and turn the bones every thirty minutes.

PREPARATION OF FRESH BONES AND FEET

Another option: Some people like an "older" look to their bones. You can achieve this by staining them with coffee. I know that you may be tempted to peroxide them until they turn brown a bit, but you have more control over it if you peroxide until white, then you may stain them to the desired result, getting them the exact color you want them.

Warning!!! Do NOT use bleach on your bones as it will damage them!

Preparing Feet

1. When prepping the feet of birds, be sure to remove the limbs right at the body or further down on the foot. The cut should be clean so that no flesh remains on the foot.

2. Fill a baking pan with salt and completely cover the feet in the salt.

PREPARATION OF FRESH BONES AND FEET

3. Set the oven's temperature to right above warm (about 200 degrees) and no warmer.

4. Let the feet bake for at least four hours, checking and turning them every two hours. It will depend on how many feet and on the size of the feet as to how much time it takes for them to dry out. Check often, as you do not want to over-cook them.

5. When dried out completely, remove and cool.

6. Spray or paint with a very light coat of sealant such as acrylic or polyurethane to seal and preserve.

7. Decorate if desired.

OR

1. Fill pan with ½ inch borax.

2. Place feet in pan of borax.

3. Cover in another ½ inch borax.

PREPARATION OF FRESH BONES AND FEET

4. Let set for a month until dry.

5. Spray or paint with a very light coat of sealant such as acrylic or polyurethane to seal and preserve.

6. Decorate if desired.

BASIC BEGINNER READING

The following is a step-by-step guide on how to do a basic reading. Keep in mind that this is a general reading and not one of the more advanced readings as discussed further in this book:

1. The Querent picks out a piece to represent himself/herself for the reading. If desired, have him/her pick out representations for other people he/she would like to include in the reading. The Querent must hold the pieces in his/her hands and concentrate as to who each piece represents, while showing them to the Ancestors, Spirit Guides, and Deities.

2. Clean bones with Florida Water, Rose Water, Hoyt's Cologne, or Sage. As mentioned earlier, it is very important not to clean the bones after the reading. If you put them away damp, they will mildew. Note that you may spray at least twelve inches away, directly on bones or spray the hands of the Querent and have them lightly clean the bones with their hands. Do not forget the cowrie shells and the "self" pieces because they are usually set aside at the beginning of the reading and sometimes get overlooked.

3. The Querent mixes the bones by turning them in the container or swishing them in a basket while meditating on a particular subject or the desire for a general knowledge. At the same time,

BASIC BEGINNER READING

the Reader raises energy with rattles, drums, or other instruments.

4. The Querent blows onto the bones. The Reader may have the Querent blow once or three times, depending on preference.

5. The Querent and the Reader both place their hands on the container or basket, both meditate and say a silent prayer asking for guidance. My personal prayer is as follows:

"Dear Lord and Lady, Great Spirit, Ancient Ones, and Ancestors, please help me see the answers to the questions this Querent so does seek. I claim this is, So Mote It Be!"

6. The Reader carefully throws the bones onto the cloth or surface by hands, container, or basket. If necessary, the Querent closes his/her eyes and carefully spreads the bones three times in a counterclockwise, circular motion, using his/her dominant hand. I have many pieces in my set, and I usually have to do this due to the surface area not being big enough. The circular motion also helps to open up communication with the spirits.

7. Concentrate on and study the throw. Look carefully at the pieces surrounding the Querent, the starter piece, the bracelet, and the Herkimer diamond (if you have them). Do not rush this process. Get a feel for what the bones are trying to say. The

BASIC BEGINNER READING

Querent and the other pieces that represent people are the most important. The bones surrounding each representation affects that person the most. The starter piece is also very important, as this is your place to begin your reading. The bracelet and Herkimer diamond are important, but optional.

8. Put up any bones that strayed. You may also collect bones that are "not speaking". (Pieces that are turned over are silent and considered "not speaking" unless otherwise noted. They will be left out of the reading.) For beginning Readers, it is important to remove the silent pieces so that the Reader may concentrate on the pieces that are speaking. For those bones which are hard to tell which side is the speaking side, place a black dot on the silent side; therefore, it eliminates all confusion. Otherwise, if you are reading every single bone in every reading, your readings will seem to be alike. With practice, you will not have to remove the silent pieces.

Note that in some cultures, it is considered rude to touch the bones during a reading. I have mixed feelings regarding this and believe it is the Reader's choice. Personally, I use an African porcupine quill for moving and touching the bones. I also have a buffalo pick for the Querent if they need to point out and ask about a group or piece.

BASIC BEGINNER READING

9. Start with the "self" piece, looking for clusters and groupings. At first, you may use the dividers to help see the groupings. With practice, you will not need the dividers and will notice the clusters right away. Feel confident to depend on your intuition for seeing your groupings.

10. Begin your reading with the bones surrounding the Querent's piece which are what is affecting the Querent the most. You might want to then turn your attention to the other pieces that represent people for the Querent, or you may want to save them and read them with the flow of the reading.

BASIC BEGINNER READING

11. Next, go to your "starter" piece. This is a piece (bone, shell, or curio of the Reader's choice) which gives the Reader a starting point.

12. If you have them, move on to the pieces inside the bracelet and then to the pieces around the Herkimer diamond. At this point, you should start to recognize what the primary points are of the reading.

13. Now, you have two choices of how to approach your throw. You can go back to your starter piece and read the clusters near it, moving circular and inward, OR you can move directly to your subject bones and their surrounding clusters. My personal preference is to first pay attention to the main subjects. I then read detailed clusters that contain no subject but are supportive to the reading. If I am doing a quick reading, I just hit the main points. Before closing, I ask the Querent if there is anything that resonates with them about the throw. I read the pieces they are referring to and begin to close the reading.

14. For clearer readings, ask questions during the reading. The Querent may use cowrie shells during the reading for yes/no answers to clarify interpretations on what each cluster is pertaining to. The Querent mixes the shells above the cluster at

BASIC BEGINNER READING

least three times while concentrating on the cluster and asking a yes/no question. if the majority of shells land with the open or slit side showing, the answer is "Yes." If the majority of shells land with the closed or smooth side showing, the answer is "No." If shells land two up and two down, it neutralizes the result. If neutral is the result, either rephrase the question or accept that the answer is unsure at that very moment. If neutral continues to show up, cleanse the shells again of all existing energy, and start over. If after three throws the answer is still neutral, you must move on. The bones are not ready to give you that information, or it may mean that you need to clean the cowrie shells again. Even if they are not used during the reading itself, always try to use cowries at the end to complete the reading.

15. Close with thanking the Ancient Ones, Spirit Guides, and Deities for their care and assistance.

16. You may anoint the Querent with essential oil to bless him/her. This is also referred to as the "Crowning".

It is important for me to mention here that I highly recommend journaling, especially in the beginning. This will help keep your thoughts organized while you are reading. It gives you a reference for questions asked during the reading. It also provides

BASIC BEGINNER READING

a record of your readings, so if a Querent comes back later, you have information at your fingertips that may help during the next reading you do for that particular Querent. I do not usually use a journal when I am doing multiple reads, such as if I am reading at an event; however, I always journal after a reading for my regular clients.

OTHER READINGS

Remember when doing the following readings, always apply steps one through eight as mentioned in Chapter 8. Remember, however, you must decide on which type of reading you want to do first, depending on the questions and the needs of the Querent.

No matter the type of reading that is being done, always try to use cowrie shells during the reading. You should at least use them at the end of the reading. Doing this clarifies any questions the Querent may have regarding each section of the reading.

At this point, you will probably have many pieces in your kit. You may choose to remove any pieces that do not pertain to the Querent or the Querent's type of reading. Remove these before cleaning the bones.

SIMPLE YES/NO READING

Use cowrie shells for quick yes or no answers. The Querent should concentrate on each question while holding the cowrie  shells and then throwing them. As stated earlier, if the majority of shells land with the open or slit side showing, the answer is "Yes." If the majority of shells land with the closed or smooth side

OTHER READINGS

showing, the answer is "No." If shells land two up and two down, it neutralizes the result. If neutral is the result, either rephrase the question or accept that the answer is unsure at that very moment. If neutral continues to show up, cleanse the shells again of all existing energy, and start over. My personal preference is to toss three times for each question, with the result being true for two out of three throws. Some only do the throw once for the result.

DAILY/WEEKLY QUICK READING

There are two ways to do a daily/weekly reading – general or subject. First, establish if the reading is for one day or one week. Daily is best because you have immediate results and advice that will affect you right away. Second, decide if the reading is a subject reading and if it is, decide what subject it is for. Examples might be love, money, legal issues, and so on.

You may want to remove the time period dice or leave it in. Just remember it does not pertain to this reading and is silent.

Throw all bones. Only read the pieces surrounding the Querent. Then, move to the pieces surrounding the starter piece. Next, read the pieces inside the bracelet. Finish by reading the pieces around the Herkimer diamond. If you do not have the

OTHER READINGS

bracelet or the Herkimer diamond, you can still do the reading. It just will not give as much information. Notice that these are the same pieces used in the technique at the start of the basic beginner reading. If a subject reading is desired, you should then read the pieces located around the particular subject in mind; however, you must make that decision before the throw so that the Querent may concentrate on that particular subject.

When doing these two types of readings, a journal is imperative if reading for yourself or regular clients! You will need to reflect back on it from time to time and will need a record for doing so.

SIMPLE SUBJECT OR FOCUS READING

In this type of reading you remove all subject pieces except the one pertaining to the subject of the Querent's choice, but make sure you continue to include the Ancestors piece and the Spirit Guide piece. You may find that two or three subject pieces may be applicable for this type of reading, and that is acceptable. For example, if doing a love/romance reading, you might use the raccoon baculum (relationships and fidelity) and ring (commitment). Remember to assign a piece to represent the Querent. This may apply to a person or group of people instead of

OTHER READINGS

a subject, but all non-applicable subject pieces must still be removed. The entire reading applies to that one topic. This reading is very similar to the Complete Subject Reading technique, which is covered later in this chapter, in that you use that style, but only focus on the one subject. You can do this for any subject. If the Querent chooses a subject that you do not have a piece to represent, use a neutral piece to temporarily represent that subject. Have the Querent concentrate on the piece and present it to the Ancestors and Spirit Guides as a representation of the subject that the Querent wishes to focus on. Note that this applies to all readings. You may refer back to Chapter 3 for a list of the most common subjects.

Throw all bones. Read the pieces surrounding the Querent, starter piece, pieces within the bracelet, and the Herkimer diamond, then move directly to the subject piece and read the surrounding pieces. Work your way around the mat to cover how the Querent will be affected by, react to, or behave towards this subject. This is a much more detailed reading than the daily/weekly subject reading, and it extends through longer periods of time.

OTHER READINGS

COMPLETE SUBJECT READING

The Complete Subject Reading is my general reading of choice and is very similar to your Basic Beginner Reading. The difference is that after reading the Querent, the starter piece, the pieces within the bracelet, and the Herkimer diamond, the Reader goes straight to subject pieces. Subjects may be read in any order. Make sure to cover all subjects and to only read the closely surrounding pieces. When finished with the last subject piece, go back through and read the pieces further around the subjects for details. At this point, you will see how the subjects flow together. End your reading by asking the Querent if there are any other areas on the spread that they feel connected to or any further questions they may have. If they want to explore a subject more, you may pull out all applicable pieces and use just them in a throw to clarify the question.

OTHER READINGS

For example, if that Querent has further questions on love and commitment of his/her marriage, you would probably choose to throw the two pieces representing the Querent and his/her spouse, the raccoon baculum, the ring, the friendship piece, the conflict piece, and collaboration. Truth and fidelity come to mind as well.

PAST, PRESENT, FUTURE

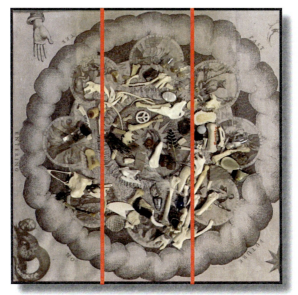

This way of reading is very self-explanatory. If your mat does not have one already designed on it, imagine a circle or square on your mat, and divide it into three vertical sections.

Throw all bones. The left section represents things of the Querent's past. The middle section represents things in the

OTHER READINGS

Querent's present. The right side represents things in the Querent's future. Begin with the left side and move toward the right to do the reading. If the "Self" piece is located within the left section, read around it first, then proceed to move on to other pieces in the section. If the "Self" piece is not in the left section, begin with the starter piece, the pieces inside the bracelet, or the Herkimer diamond, but completely read the left section first. Move on to the center section, repeating the process. Finally, read the right section. NOTE: No matter where the beginner pieces fall, always read from left to right!

LONG DISTANCE READING

To do a long-distance reading, you will throw the bones over a photo of the Querent or over the Querent's name and birth date written on a paper. This forms a connection between the Querent, the Reader, and the Ancestors.

Simply place the photo or name and birth date underneath the center of your mat. You may now begin the desired type of reading.

OTHER READINGS

DECISION READING

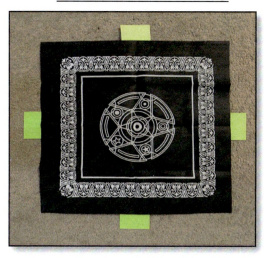

I learned this type of reading from the book <u>Bones, Shells, and Curios</u> by Michele Jackson, which is a book I highly recommend for both the beginner and the advanced Reader.

Use a square mat. The Querent may choose up to four options for a particular decision to be made. Write each choice on a separate piece of paper and place each one under the edge of each side of the mat.

Throw all bones. After throwing the bones, read the pieces close to each choice to determine the outcome for each decision. Ignore subject pieces unless applicable, because you are focusing on supporting bones. Choose your best outcome!

OTHER READINGS

RELATIONSHIP READING

(Love, Friends, Family, Work)

Assign a piece for the Querent and each person the Querent wants included in the reading. If multiple people are included, assign multiple pieces. This type of reading works best if you do only two people at a time.

After throwing the bones, look on the pieces directly around the assigned "people" pieces. Next, concentrate on the subject piece(s) associated with the type of relationship. For example, with love, if a romantic reading, read the raccoon baculum and ring, and their surrounding pieces. If it is a friendship reading, read the subject piece that represents friendship and the pieces surrounding it. At this point you might want to consider reading other subject pieces. For example as stated above, the ring piece represents commitment and a friendship is a commitment. Is this piece speaking to you in this reading? If so, use it in the reading. If the conflict piece lands near the subject piece, you may want to explore that. Look around the throw to read any piece which is speaking to you. You may end the reading at this point.

OTHER READINGS

CIRCLE WITHIN CIRCLE READING

Ignore the traditional beginning pieces of Querent, starter, bracelet, and Herkimer. The entire reading is about the Querent, so it is redundant to have those pieces in there. Throw all bones.

Any piece that falls within the center circle affects the Querent directly. Any piece that falls out of the center circle but within the larger one affects the Querent indirectly. Pieces that fall outside the larger circle are silent and do not speak to the Querent at all.

TRADITIONAL READING – "SUN CROSS" METHOD

OTHER READINGS

This reading uses the cross inside a circle, known as a sun cross mat, marking for direction. You will look at pieces within each half of the circle to direct your reading. If you do not have a mat designed for this method, imagine a circle divided into quarters like a pie. Also, if you do not have a sun cross mat, you may use two pieces of string after the throw to make the cross like quartering out a pizza. Another idea is to draw a cross on a sheet of paper and lay it on your mat before the throw. I suggest either purchasing a mat or making one of your own. If it is for you only, it is not so important. If reading for a client, you want to look professional.

The beginning pieces do not apply to this reading either. Throw all bones. The upper half of the circle represents things that the Querent clearly sees. It is the conscious part of the reading. The lower half of the circle represents things that the Querent cannot completely see. It is the subconscious level of the reading. The left side of the circle represents things of the Querent's past. The right side of the circle represents things in the Querent's future.

OTHER READINGS

DIRECTIONAL READING

This reading is great to use for one subject or area of the Querent's life, particularly new projects and goals, but it may also be used for an all-purpose or general reading. Again, the piece representing the Querent will not be used, because the whole reading is for him/her.

The Querent decides on what the reading is about, whether specific or general. The Querent communicates to the Reader what the reading is going to be about. This reading is similar to a tarot reading, due to its relationships to the directions and elements. It is the most complicated of the readings.

After the Querent chooses what the reading is about, it is common to remove all subject pieces not pertaining to the throw. My preference is to keep all pieces in to see how they will be affected.

The Querent and Reader focus on what the reading is about and how it relates to the Querent. Make it clear which sections on the mat represent which direction – use East, South, West, and North directions and their elements (earth, air, fire, and water) along with their corresponding representations (thoughts, actions,

OTHER READINGS

development/feelings, and tangibles).

Throw all bones.

We start with East, which represents thoughts. The bones in this section represent the Querent's thoughts and concerns, including future events.

We then move on to South because it represents action. It focuses on actions and work. The bones in this section refer to actions and work that needs to be taken to manifest the desired result.

Next, we go to West, because it represents development of the work or action itself. Feelings are also included here. This area focuses on the work and gestation needing to move on to the next phase.

Finally, we move on to North, which represents tangible things. It is here that we see the results. If the results are not the desired result of the Querent, he/she will be able to refer to this reading to make changes to achieve his/her goals. The other directions are used for guidance suggestions to get us here at the final result. If all other directions are followed as is, this area represents what stands as it is now.

OTHER READINGS

You might include Spirit, located in the center, to represent the collection as a whole and to see what is directly affecting the Querent in this reading.

This reading can get a little confusing at times, so I like to provide my students with a little story that shows the representations of the directions:

> **A person is in the East and is thinking of taking a test. He/she travels to the South to take the test. Next, he/she is in the West waiting for the development of the test. Here feelings are brought out as well as possibilities. Finally, he/she moves North, and the results of the test is given!**

If the outcome of this reading is not the desired one, use the Decision Reading to figure out what to do to change the outcome. Cowries are very important during this reading to use throughout in order to clarify.

OTHER READINGS

There are many readings to choose from depending on your Querent's circumstances. Just remember that the Beginner Basic Reading; the Complete Subject Reading; the Past, Present, Future Reading; the Circle Within a Circle Reading; the Sun Cross Method; and the Directional Readings are similar as far as general readings. Choose the one that resonates with you best and develop that one more than the others. However, the other readings are still necessary to learn because they are for particular situations, and you will use them often.

CONCLUSION

As you see, there is much to "throwing bones;" however, it does not have to be intimidating or discouraging. If you learn a little bit about its past and follow some simple instructions, you can form a connection and enter into a beautiful relationship with them.

This form of divination is very personal and intimate in that it relies on the relationships you have with your Ancestors, Spirit Guides, and Deities. Over time, you will develop these relationships and will have the confidence to read for yourself and others.

RESOURCES

Online Stores to Acquire Bones

Hillbilly Furniture and Furs

Contact: Misty Lane

207-672-6702

Mistylane13@gmail.com

www.Hillbillyfurnitureandfurs.com

Coupon code: "Throwbones" 10% off

The Bone Room

Contact: Diana Mansfield

510-526-5252

boneroom@gmail.comv

https://www.boneroom.com

RESOURCES

The Skull Store

(416) 363-1060

BuySkulls@gmail.com

https://www.skullstore.ca

Metaphysical

The Craft: A Hair Studio & Metaphysical Shoppe

Contact: Priestess Tiffany Lee

154 Laurens St NW, Aiken, SC 29801

(803) 295-6616

Coupon code: "Throwthebones" 10% off

RESOURCES

Outre

Contact: Lisa Luna

lisaluna1969@gmail.com

256-424-3147

Etsy Shop OutreSacredMoon

Coupon code: "Thembones" 10% off

REFERENCES

Michele Jackson; Bones, Shells, and Curios; The Lucky Mojo Curio Company; 2014

Catherine Yronwode; Throwing the Bones; Lucky Mojo Curio Company; 2012

Cindy Rhodes; Throwing the Bones; 2019

Stephanie Rose Bird, Sticks, Stones, Roots, & Bones, Llewellyn Publications, 2017

http://www.thewhitegoddess.co.uk

https://www.carolinaconjure.com

https://archaichoney.com

https://en.wikipedia.org/wiki/Scapulimancy

http://www.oldstyleconjure.com

https://readersandrootworkers.org

https://en.wikipedia.org/wiki/Oracle_bone

https://www.ancient.eu/Oracle_Bones/

https://www.britannica.com/science/sangoma

https://eshowe.com/zulu-sangoma/

https://www.jstor.org/stable/40979537?seq=1#page_scantab_contents

http://www.sundaystandard.info/batswana-still-strongly-believe-dingaka-tsa-setswana

PERSONAL IMPRESSIONS

Use this space to record your thoughts and feelings when casting your bones.

PERSONAL IMPRESSIONS

PERSONAL IMPRESSIONS

PERSONAL IMPRESSIONS